Advanced Foot Control
For Dancers

Written By Lisa Howell

Disclaimer

The contents of this manual, including text, graphics, images, and other material are for informational purposes only, and is provided as an accompaniment to the online video course. Nothing contained in this manual is or should be considered or used as a substitute for professional medical or health advice, diagnosis, or treatment. The information provided in this report is provided on an "as is" basis, without any warranty, express or implied.

Never disregard medical advice from any treating doctor or other qualified health care provider or delay seeking advice because of something you have read in this document. We urge that dancers seek the advice of a physician or other qualified health professional with any questions they may have regarding a medical or health condition. In case of emergency, please call your doctor immediately.

The Ballet Blog holds no liability or responsibility for any injury or complication that may arise from following this information. Any use of this manual is voluntary and at your own risk. If you require further information about any injury, please feel free to contact us to organise an individual consultation either in person or via Skype/Phone.

Published 2018 by The Ballet Blog - Third Edition (First 2008. Second 2011)

© Copyright The Ballet Blog 2018

ALL RIGHTS RESERVED

Except for the purpose of fair reviewing, no part of this publication may be reproduced or transmitted in any form or by any means, electronic or mechanical, including photocopying, recording or any information storage and retrieval system, without prior written permission from the publisher.

Contents

Introduction 5
    Overview of the Course 6
    Anatomy of the Pointed Foot 7
    Foot Massage Techniques 8

Anatomy and Activation Exercises 13
    Bones of the Foot and Lower Leg 14
    Arches of the Foot 18
    Gastrocnemius 20
    Soleus 27
    Achilles Tendon 35
    The Peroneals 41
    Tibialis Anterior 50
    Tibialis Posterior 56
    Lumbricals and Interossei 62
    Flexor Hallucis Longus (FHL) 70
    Flexor Hallucis Brevis (FHB) 71
    Flexor Digitorum Longus (FDL) 78
    Summary 84

Related Resources 87

Introduction

The Advanced Foot Control course is a follow-on from our original book for dancers called 'The Perfect Pointe Book', which teaches the basic anatomy and understanding behind training the dancers foot, and prepares the whole body for progressing onto pointe. Once you have grasped the basics of working your feet and ankles correctly you can start to do some more specific and targeted exercise to further improve your strength and control. This is especially important if you are starting to learn harder steps en pointe, performing in bare feet at a high level or recovering from injury.

In this book we go into a lot more detail about the anatomy of the foot as you need to know it from a dancers point of view, whether you are a student or a teacher, or even a therapist learning to work with dancers.

We will not discuss EVERY muscle in the foot in this course, just the ones that you really need. It is very important for any dancer to learn about the anatomy of their feet and ankles, and what they are designed to do. If the muscles in the feet and ankles are not working in their optimal way, the alignment of the bones in the foot and the biomechanical function of the foot may suffer. Often we can carry minor weaknesses for a long time without realising that anything is wrong, however when the foot is stressed more the strain begins to be felt. This often happens just before performances or exams when you have increased rehearsals, and need your feet the most!

While you do not need to know all of the details of exactly where each muscle attaches - as we go through the program try and create a mental picture of where the muscle lies and how it is designed to move your foot. Sometimes it takes a little while to learn the names of these muscles, however it does make sense when you learn how they are named (included in the description of each muscle). Learning this will make it much easier to talk about them with any therapists you may have to see in your dancing career.

Overview of the Course

For each muscle that we discuss in the course we will look first at its anatomy, from a dancers point of view. We will then go through some graded activation and strengthening exercises, and then finally some massage and stretching ideas to help release any excess tension that may be building up. By following this program, you will soon begin to feel very differently about your feet, and how they can help you in your dancing.

Anatomy of the Pointed Foot

Learning how to use all of the muscles in your feet and ankles is essential to all dancers, whether you do Classical Ballet, Contemporary Dance, Jazz, Latin or Ballroom styles. This is because all of the muscles in your feet and ankle are designed to do a certain job. If they are all working correctly then your feet will feel great and can function at their full capacity.

However, in many dancers these muscles do not work exactly as they are designed to. Often isolated weaknesses in the feet can go unnoticed for some time, as the body is very good at substituting other muscles to fill in for those that are not pulling their own weight. However, over time the muscles that are substituting begin to get fatigued and may start developing overuse injuries or get sore from working too much. It is like someone trying to work a day shift and night shift for months on end. It will be ok in the beginning, but is not a great long term strategy!

When we look at how it all should work, you should be able to pointe the ankles primarily with your big calf muscles - Gastrocnemius and Soleus. These are large powerful muscles that can generate a lot of force. The deeper muscles in the calf are called Extrinsic Foot Muscles and have long tendons crossing the ankle. These muscles are designed to control the position of the ankle and stabilise you when the foot is flat as well as on demi-pointe and full pointe. The Intrinsic Foot Muscles are all of the small muscles that start and end within the foot. These muscles are the ones that control the arches of the feet, and point the toes correctly.

If one or two muscles are not performing correctly, others get overworked. For example: If the big calf muscles and the intrinsic foot muscles are not working effectively, the extrinsic foot muscles may become overloaded as they attempt to perform all three roles. This result may in irritation, pain and sometimes clicking in the tendons that pass around the back of the ankle.

This book is designed to help you train all of your foot muscles correctly so that you can get the most out of your feet, and enjoy a long and injury free career in dance!

Foot Massage Techniques

Massage has been used for thousands of years to relax the body and to increase mobility. Unfortunately as manual therapists such as Physiotherapists, Osteopaths and Massage Therapists have become more qualified and the industry has become regulated many people are scared of touching each other if they have not been formally trained.

Touch is a very natural and healing practice, and with a little sense and sensibility, you do not need years of training to be able to get good effect from your "treatments". While you can do all of these techniques yourself, I often teach parents how to help their dancing children by massaging their feet, neck and shoulders, and everyone seems to enjoy this. I also often recommend a "contra-deal" system to trade treatments for a neck massage that is usually well needed by ballet mums or dancing friends!

If you are feeling restricted in your foot and ankle range, or simply want to develop more mobility, there are many simple massage techniques in this book that can help you unlock your true potential.

If you are serious about dancing as a career I recommend enrolling in a short massage course to get comfortable with using your hands on yourself and others. Go with a friend and then trade a treatment with them once a week or so. This can be a great way to keep trouble spots looser, and while it is not a replacement for seeking medical assistance when needed, it can keep you dancing pain-free for longer.

While massage can be extremely beneficial there are a few precautions that you need to be aware of, so please follow all of the instructions carefully. Here are the answers to some common questions that usually come up when we teach the course as a workshop.

How hard do I go?

It is not necessary to use huge amounts of pressure to get some dramatic effects with hands on massage techniques for your feet. When you first begin, go gently and monitor the effect afterwards. You may "feel" the muscles that you have been working on, however there should never be any pain following treatment. Gradually increase the intensity of your 'treatments' until you get the desired effect. Effective treatment should result in an immediate feeling of ease of movement if applied to the correct muscles.

Why is it different on one side compared to the other?

Just as you are often stronger and more flexible on one side compared to the other, you will often feel a different level of tension in the same muscles on either foot. Make note of what you feel, and over time you should be able to balance out the tension a little more.

What areas should I NOT do? Can I do any damage?

There are a few exposed nerves along the undersurface of the foot and around the ankle, so it is important that you do not push into any area that gives pain into an area other than the one you are pressing on or any tingling or 'shooting' sensations. We will discuss each of these areas as we work through the course. Also, only ever massage above and below an injury, rather than right over where it is sore, unless instructed by your therapist. Do not push into pain and you will not cause damage to your feet. It is important to always monitor exactly what you are feeling under your fingers as well as what you are feeling internally.

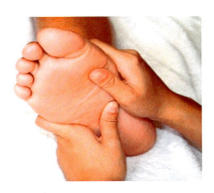

My thumbs hurt afterwards. What should I do?

If you are quite mobile in your hands you may find it hard to keep your thumbs aligned properly while treating your feet. It is very important that you do not hyperextend your joints while massaging the feet as the ligaments in your hands are very delicate. Fortunately you do not always have to use your thumbs! You can also use your knuckles, elbows and various balls or other firm objects to massage tension out of your muscles. It is very important that you take care when using other implements to massage as you do not have the same feedback sensations as when you use your own hands.

When is the best time for massaging the feet?

There are two different reasons why you may be massaging your feet, and as such there are two different times that I recommend to work on them. If you want to increase your range, then this is best done away from class time, on a day that you do not have ballet. The feet should be warm, ideally after a foot bath so that the tissues are softer to work with, however as you will be going a little deeper with these techniques I would not do this after a tough class. The second reason you may want to massage the feet is to recover after a demanding class. This type of treatment should be much more gentle and focused on moving fluid from the feet. This is obviously done after class, and may be preceded and followed by an ice bath to reduce any inflammation. I recommend at least twice weekly treatments for full time dancers, and it is good to do deep treatments on a day when you are not dancing so much.

What cream should I use?

You can use many different creams or moisturisers for massaging. Creams with Arnica (A natural herbal treatment) in them are also good and may help to reduce inflammation and pain. Massage oil is sometimes too slippery and light moisturisers absorb quickly. You need a reasonably thick cream to get a good balance of resistance and slide for optimal results. I like to use our "International Rub" (available on the online shopping cart on www.theballetblog.com) which has a lovely peppermint scent, especially great when treating smelly feet!

What else can I do to take care of my feet?

After a heavy class it is a good idea to soak the feet in a bucket of iced water for 10 – 15 minutes. This acts like an ice pack, chilling down your feet, closing down all of the small blood vessels and reducing swelling. This can help prevent chronic injuries where inflammation builds up over a period of time. After chilling the feet down, elevate them (put them up a wall) for 10 -20 minutes to help the fluid return into your lymphatic system.

Reflexology for dancers

Chinese medicine doctors have been using reflexology points for thousands of years to treat all kinds of complaints. It can be an interesting experience to have a reflexology session with a good practitioner to learn about what each tight area means in that system of medicine. This can be quite enlightening, and you may find some extra points that you can treat yourself. Often releasing points in your feet can have a beneficial effect on your flexibility as well!

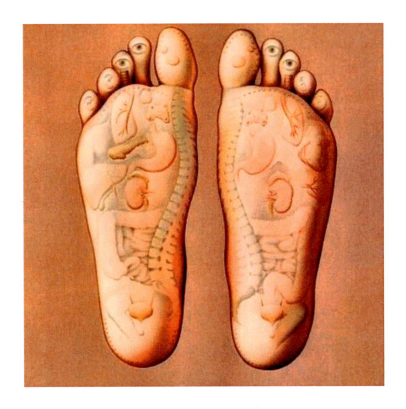

Notes:

Anatomy and Activation Exercises

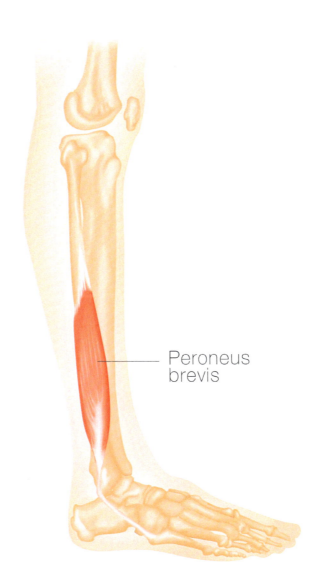

Bones of the Foot and Lower Leg

As Leonardo da Vinci said "The human foot is a masterpiece of engineering and a work of art." When working properly, it allows us to run, jump and dance in the most extraordinary ways. The many bones of the foot are organised in a way to allow shock absorption, dynamic propulsion and balance in all kinds of positions. Unfortunately however, things can go wrong especially in the dancer who demands so much of her feet. But before we begin to learn about the muscles in the lower leg, we need to have a concept of how the bones of the foot are organised to enable it to perform all of the functions that we demand of it.

There are two bones of the lower leg: the Tibia and the Fibula, and there is a strong membrane that connects them called the Interosseous Membrane. Many muscles that move the foot and toes actually attach to this membrane high in the lower leg, and then feed down into the foot. We call these our Extrinsic Foot Muscles.

Then there are the Tarsal (Foot) Bones. The biggest of these is the heel bone, or Calcaneus. It is very important that the heel bone is kept in a good alignment, as if it begins to tilt in, it sets all of the muscles that are around the ankle at an odd angle.

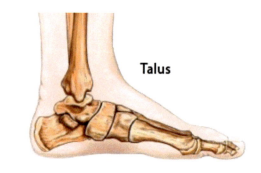

The Talus is a very important tarsal bone in a classical dancer. It is a pivotal bone in the foot as it connects to the tibia and fibula, the Calcaneus and to the bones of the mid foot. If any of the joints that the Talus is involved with are restricted, then we can feel restriction in the movement at the ankle.

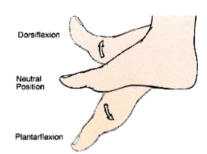

The Joint between the Tibia and Fibula and the top of the Talus is the Talocrural Joint. This joint needs to be quite mobile in dancers to allow full range of motion in the ankle. If it is restricted you may notice a reduced pointe range or feel pain or restriction at the front of the ankle en fondu, rather than a stretch up the back of the ankle.

The Joint between the Talus and the Calcaneus is called the Subtalar Joint. If this joint is restricted you may find it hard to balance on one foot, as it is the joint that adjusts sideways to help us balance on one leg. You may also find it hard to 'fish' your foot when pointing, or get told off for 'sickling'. This joint often stiffens up after a bad ankle sprain but this frequently goes unnoticed as it will not be painful.

The Tarsal Bones also include the Cuboid, Navicular, and three Cuneiform bones. These bones help shape the inner arch of the foot and are very important in transferring forces through the foot. The joints between them are often very stiff in people who get stress fractures of the foot and lower leg. The Metatarsals are the long bones of the foot and the Phalanges are all of the little toe bones.

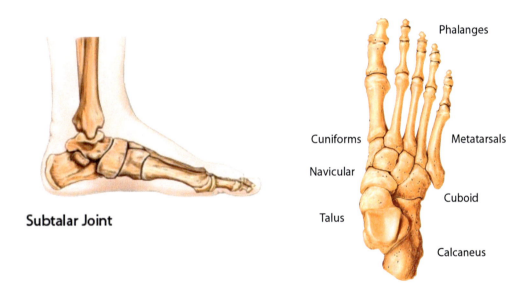

Mid Foot Mobility

There are many bones in the foot that can cause restriction in range; however we are going to focus on mobilising just two areas – The joint between the rear and mid-foot, and the joints between the mid-foot and forefoot. Restriction in these areas can restrict the arch through the middle of the foot.

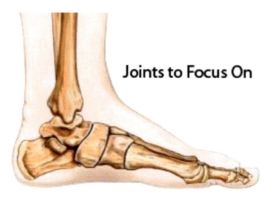

Joints to Focus On

1. Sit on the floor with your left leg to the front, turned out with the knee bent. Tuck your right leg behind you. Use your left hand to hold the back part of the left foot firmly with your thumb on the sole of the foot and the fingers over the front of the ankle. Place the right hand very close to the left, again with the thumb under the arch and the fingers over the top of the foot.

2. Grasping the foot firmly with your left hand, rotate the middle of the foot with your right hand as though you are wringing out a cloth, to twist the foot at the level between the rearfoot/midfoot joint.

3. Repeat further down the foot, at the top of the big toe bone, marking the division between the midfoot and forefoot.

Notes:

Arches of the Foot

The foot is designed in such a way that it has 3 dynamic arches. 'Dynamic' means that they are designed to move and flex as we move, rather than being held in one place all the time. We have one arch down the outer border of the foot, one down the inner border, and one across the middle of the forefoot. These arches are supported by complex slings of muscles and fascia that work together to create flexibility, spring and cushioning in the foot.

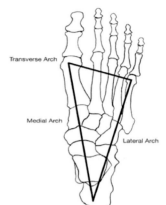

However, when most people talk of a dancers arches, they are referring to the arch along the inner border of the foot – the medial arch. Some people have a flat arch, others have a high arch, and some have one in between. The appearance of the arch can be due to either the shape of the bones, or muscle control, or both!

Some dancers (and people in general) will have the appearance of a 'flat foot' due to having very mobile ligaments and poor muscular support. This kind of mobile foot can be developed to look great when very strong, however this kind of foot can suffer from lots of injuries if it is weak. This foot often looks reasonable (or even very good) in a demi-pointe position, however the shape of the arch drops as the dancer lowers her heel. Specific strengthening of the arch is essential before commencing pointe work or a lot of allegro. Other dancers do have anatomically 'flat feet' which is identified by a flatter curve to their arch in standing due to the actual shape of the bones in their foot. No matter how strong the small foot muscles get, the shape of the foot will not change significantly. This foot will look flat along the inner arch without the heel bone rolling in, and often will still look flat when placed on demi-pointe. It is still important that we focus on strengthening this kind of foot, but we must not expect dramatic changes in the shape of the arch.

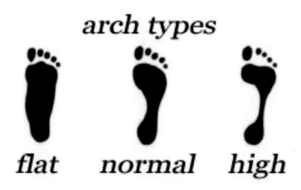

Some dancers may appear to have a very high arch in their foot, and often they get told that they have 'strong feet', however they can still be very weak in the small muscles of the feet. A high inner arch is often created by stiff ligaments holding the arch rigidly in place, without any muscular support.

While it may appear that the dancer has good control of the arch as it does not roll in en fondu, it is important to make sure that the foot has the mobility and strength to cope with the demands of dance. If there is little movement between the bones en fondu these dancers can be prone to foot, ankle and knee injuries due to the lack of shock absorption in allegro and pointe work.

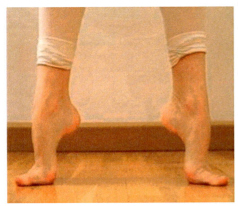

The dancer must be able to maintain a good position of the rear foot when standing in parallel, in turnout and en fondu. During petit allegro there should be good dynamic control of the arches to demonstrate adequate control of any shaped foot. In any of these foot types weakness in the muscles that support the arches of the foot can place unnecessary and constant strain on the plantar fascia. This is the most common cause of pain in the sole of the foot, and strengthening of all of the muscles that support the arches must be included in any rehabilitation program.

It is essential that each dancer learn the strengthening exercises relative to his or her type of foot, and be aware of the implications of their body type before progressing to full time dance training or pointe work. Even people who have always been told that they have 'Good Feet' often need specific strengthening work to make the most of them!

Gastrocnemius

Gastrocnemius is the anatomical name for your big calf muscles. The muscle has two 'heads' that attach to the thigh bone (Femur) just above the knee. These then attach into the Achilles Tendon at the back of the ankle. While this is obviously an essential muscle for a dancer, it is astounding how many dancers have problems with the timing and weakness in this muscle.

Origin:
By two 'heads' from either side of the thigh bone (Femur) just above the knee.

Insertion:
Via a strong tendon (Achilles Tendon) into the heel bone (Calcaneus)

Action:
When the knee is straight Gastrocnemius points the ankle (plantarflexion), however since it also crosses the knee joint, the Gastrocnemius can assist in bending the knee (knee flexion) when the foot is flexed.

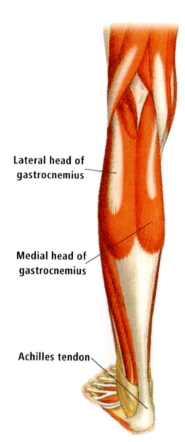

The Gastrocnemius is very important in normal walking to get an effective push off. It is also essential in pointing the foot and for allegro (jumping). However, if it is not supported correctly by the other muscles that assist these actions, the calf may become overloaded. Some dancers will display an over developed Gastrocnemius if their deeper calf muscles are not working properly.

However, one of the most common issues with the Gastrocnemius in dancers is delayed timing and poor recruitment of the Medial Gastrocnemius. This is easily observed during rises and by feeling the muscle on the inner part of the calf. Most people will be able to find this muscle simply by focusing on it, however sometimes we need to use Electronic Muscular Stimulation (EMS) to get it working!

Medial Muscle Belly Activation

This is a good way to test if the inner part of your Gastrocnemius is working or not. You may have to get a friend to feel for the contraction if you are not flexible enough to sit with your legs out in front. Having a strong Medial Gastrocnemius will help prevent lots of common foot injuries, especially overuse injuries of the smaller muscles around the ankle.

1. Place a small soft ball against the wall or a box. Sit on the floor with one leg outstretched with the ball of the foot resting on the ball. Place your fingers over the meaty part of your inner calf muscle.

2. Slowly point the ankle (keeping the toes pulled back). Take note of how strongly the muscle comes on, and at what point in the movement.

3. Aim to have it slowly come on throughout the whole range and be very firm at the end of the movement.

4. Slowly flex the ankle, gradually releasing the tension in the muscle. Make sure you do not suddenly let it relax as you release the contraction.

5. Repeat for 20 good contractions, making sure you keep your spine in a good position throughout, no slumping!

Note:
- Make sure to keep your spine straight
- The muscle should come on as you begin to point your ankle, not just at the end of the movement
- There should be no pain at the back of the ankle

Single Leg Rises

Once you have made sure that the Gastrocnemius is working efficiently, and your placement on demi-pointe is correct (by doing both Seated Rises and Double Leg Rises as in The Perfect Pointe Book), you can begin building your strength in Single Leg Rises.

For advanced level dancers, aim for 25 single leg rises in parallel on each leg every day, without adjusting your position during the set! Full time dancers should aim for 30 repetitions. A good time to practice these is when you are brushing your teeth either in the morning or at night.

1. Stand facing a chair or barre on one foot in parallel. Make sure that you knee is pulled up, but not hyper-extended. Keep the ankle of the lifted leg pointed and the toes lengthened.

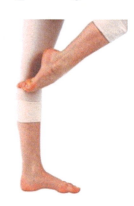

2. Slowly rise onto demi-pointe, making sure not to lean forward on the barre. Keep the toes long and the knee straight. Make sure that your hips stay aligned and your shoulders are relaxed. Keep your turnout muscles gently activated (yes, even in parallel) to keep your knee facing the front.

3. Slowly lower the heel, trying to keep the skin of the sole of the foot off the floor. Repeat 25 times, or until the calf begins to fatigue. Once you can do these well in parallel, try repeating in turnout.

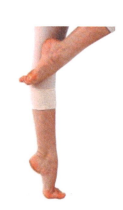

Note:
- Keep your spine straight, hips square and knee pulled up throughout
- Push straight up, don't lean forward or use momentum to rise
- Keep the foot muscles active throughout
- Don't push yourself to do 25 in the beginning. Build your strength slowly

Single Leg Rise Variations

Some people may experience pain under the ball of their foot when performing single leg rises. If your 2nd metatarsal (long toe bone) is longer than your big toe it can tend to press down on the ground and cause a little callus to form underneath. This can also happen under the big toe if it is longer than the second. Other people experience pain in the big toe with rises if the joint of the big toe is stiff. Using a carefully folded towel when practicing your rises can help to prevent any pain or inflammation in this area.

If you have pain under your second toe:

1. Use a small towel. Fold it in half length-wise then fold quarter of one end over on itself twice. Repeat this from the other end so that the two folded edges almost meet in the middle.
2. Place the folded towel in front of your barre. Stand on the towel so that your second toe falls in the gap between the two folds.
3. Try your rises in this position.

If you have pain under your big toe:

1. Start with the towel folded in half length-wise, then fold the towel into thirds.
2. Place the folded towel in front of your barre. Stand on the towel so that your big toe is on the ground and your 2nd, 3rd, 4th and 5th toes are on the towel.
3. You should be able to rise higher in this position, with no pressure in the joint.

Gastrocnemius Massage

Once you begin to use the Gastrocnemius properly in class you may find that it gets a little tight (especially if you were not using it before!). Simple massage techniques to get the blood moving, and a few trigger point releases can help remove any excess tension while you build your strength.

1. Begin by massaging the bulk of the calf muscle in large circular movements to get the blood flowing. You may use your fingers, the heel of your hand, or ask a friend to help.

2. Then, see if you can find each of the trigger points indicated in the picture to the right in your calf. Find a tight point, then gently maintain pressure on it for 15 seconds or until it starts to release. If it does not release you may be pressing too hard.

3. Repeat over several points in the big calf muscle. Follow the trigger point releases with further large circular massage movements to get the blood flowing.

Note:
- Make sure that there is no pain following the trigger point releases or massage
- Focus on consciously letting the muscle tension go, rather than forcing through it with your fingers
- If you have a calf strain, don't massage over the painful area
- Follow the massage with a gentle stretch

Gastrocnemius Stretches

Your calves can get very tight, especially if you are doing a lot of dancing. Make sure to do frequent gentle calf stretches to keep the flexibility in your calf when you are doing all of your foot exercises. As the Gastrocnemius muscle attaches above the knee, make sure to keep your knee straight when stretching it.

1. Stand with the legs in a lunge position, one foot forward and one foot back. Keep your body upright, with the legs in parallel and both heels on the floor.

2. Keep your hands on your hips to check your alignment, and then slowly bend the front knee to get a stretch in the calf of the back leg.

3. Keep breathing gently and focus on consciously relaxing the calf muscle to ease further into the stretch. Hold for 3 – 4 breaths.

4. Release the back leg, and then repeat on the other side. Repeat at least twice on each side.

Note:
- Keep both feet in parallel and the knees facing directly forward
- Breathe into the stretch, and focus on relaxing, rather than just pulling the muscle into a stretch
- There should be no pain in the calf with this stretch, keep it gentle
- There should be no pain or pinching at the front of the ankle

Notes:

Soleus

The Soleus is your deeper calf muscle that is stretched in a bent knee calf stretch and in a plié. The major roles of the Soleus are to control the ankle when landing from a jump and in pointing the ankle when the knee is flexed.

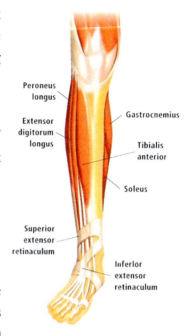

Origin:
The Soleus muscle originates from the upper parts of the back of both lower leg bones (Tibia and Fibula), and the membrane that joins them (Interosseous Membrane).

Insertion:
Inserts into the heel bone (Calcaneus) via the Achilles Tendon.

Action:
Soleus works concentrically to point the ankle especially when the knee is bent, and to push off in walking and jumping. It works eccentrically to control the flexion of the ankle (dorsiflexion) when landing from a jump.

Poor Soleus recruitment on landing results in thumping of the heels and overloading into the quadriceps. It is therefore very important to train this muscle if you have any knee issues such as Patello-Femoral Pain (PFP) and syndromes such as Osgood Schlatters Disease.

Effective control of the ankle when landing is also essential to reduce forces through the small foot bones and shins so should be assessed when rehabilitating from stress fractures and other overuse injuries.

Not using Soleus well may result in irritation of the Achilles Tendon and overuse of the long toe flexors (causing thickening and clicking of the tendons around the ankle) which may limit the depth of your demi plie, and cause pain in the back of the ankle when pointing the foot. Improving your Soleus activation can remarkably improve the range at the ankle when used during class.

Soleus Rises En Fondu

Strengthening the Soleus is very important especially when preparing for a variation that involves lots of small jumps. Regular class work rarely trains the Soleus specifically so this is a good exercise to add into your routine. Initially you may find that the movement is a little jerky, however work towards lowering the heel as smoothly as possible.

Level 1 – Double Leg In Parallel

1. Start with your feet in parallel facing the barre. Go into a demi-plié in parallel, keeping your arches on and knees over your second toe with the front of the pelvis vertical.

2. Slowly rise through the feet onto demi-pointe keeping the knees flexed.

3. Slowly lower your heels in one smooth movement (it will usually be a little bit jerky the first few times!) Repeat 10 times.

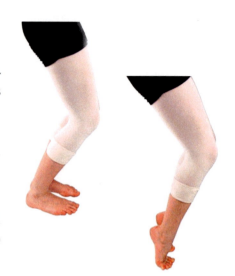

Level 2 – Double Leg In Turnout

1. Repeat with the feet in first position facing the barre. Go into a demi-plié, keeping your arches on and knees over your second toe.

2. Slowly rise through the feet onto demi-pointe keeping the knees flexed and the thighs turned out from the hips.

3. Slowly lower your heels in one smooth movement. Repeat 10 times.

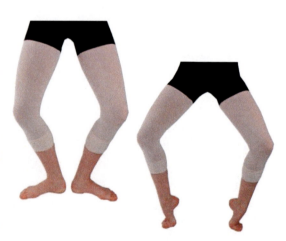

Level 3 – In Parallel with Transfer

1. Start with a demi-plié in parallel facing the barre. Slowly rise through the feet onto demi-pointe keeping the knees flexed.

2. Transfer your weight over onto one foot, still with the knee flexed. Make sure to keep the ankle fully pointed, rather than pulling back as you transfer your weight.

3. Slowly lower the heel in one smooth movement, keeping the supporting knee bent. Place the lifted foot back into parallel and straighten the legs before repeating on the other side.

Level 4 – In Turnout With Transfer

1. Demi-plié in first position facing the barre. Slowly rise through the feet onto a high demi-pointe keeping the knees flexed.

2. Transfer your weight over onto one foot, still with the knee flexed. Try to keep the front of the foot lengthened for optimal strengthening. Slowly lower the heel in one smooth movement, en fondu.

3. Place the feet back into first position and straighten the legs before repeating on the other side.

Note:
- Make sure to keep your abdominals on to keep the front of the pelvis vertical
- Keep your turnout muscles on to keep the knee aligned over the toes
- Make sure to stay high on your demi-pointe when transferring your weight to one foot

Preparation for Petit Jeté

This is a great way to integrate the strengthening of the Soleus into class work. Make sure to focus on keeping the arches gently activated as you lower your heels each time, and don't forget to use your turnout and abdominal muscles to control the alignment of the leg.

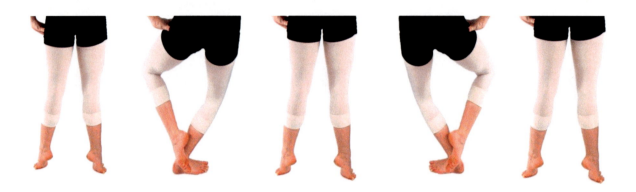

1. Start with the feet in first position facing the barre. Rise onto demi-pointe in first position, using your deep abdominals and turnout muscles to stay centred.

2. Transfer your weight to the right foot and simultaneously bend the knee and lower the heel to finish en fondu. Make sure that your arches stay lifted and your knee stays over your second toe.

3. Push back up to place both feet on demi-pointe in first position, before transferring your weight to the other foot, again lowering en fondu.

4. Repeat 8 times slowly each side, and then increase the speed of the movement to make it more fluid. Next, perform 16 fast repetitions and then perform 16 normal petits jetés, focusing on your foot and turnout control.

Note:
- Use your deep turnout muscles to keep your knee aligned over your 2nd toe as you fondu
- Keep your back vertical throughout this exercises – often dancers lean forward when landing from small jumps

Fondu Exercise on Demi-Pointe

This exercise is surprisingly difficult for some people, especially if they have very flexible ankles. If this is the case, they often lack the strength to control into their full range, and will try to stabilise the ankle by pulling back from their full range, especially en pointe. This is an essential exercise to master in order to be able to make the most of your natural range.

1. Start with your right hand on the barre, with the feet in fifth position (left foot at the front). Rise in fifth, and then pick the left foot up into sur le cou-de-pied position.

2. Fondu on the supporting leg, keeping the left foot in at the neck of the right ankle. Slowly straighten the supporting leg, unfolding the left leg to a low developpé devant, having both legs straighten at the same time.

3. Slowly bend the supporting leg again, lowering the right heel slightly, and bring the left foot back into the sur le cou-de-pied position.

4. Repeat à la seconde, derrière, and then again to seconde straightening both knees at the same time, keeping your hips level and square to the front. This exercise may also be performed with the ankle staying fully pointed as you fondu on demi pointe.

Note:
- Use your deep turnout muscles to keep your knee aligned over your 2nd toe as you fondu
- Keep looking straight ahead, not down at your feet!

Soleus Massage

If you have never really worked the Soleus muscle before it may get a little tight when you start doing some focused strengthening for it! Gentle massage can release tension and can actually help increase the activation of the muscle in some people.

1. The Soleus muscles responds best to a combination of trigger point releases and small circular movements to get the blood flowing. See if you can find each of the trigger points indicated in your calf. This can take some practise but is worth it when you get the right spot!

2. Find the point; hold it firmly for 15 seconds and it should start to release. If it doesn't, you are holding too hard. Repeat on several points. Aim to feel the muscle relaxing under your hand, rather than just aiming to feel pain!

3. Then massage the bulk of the muscle in sweeping movements to get the blood flowing again.

Note:
- Try not to feel like you are pushing the muscle out of the way
- Focus on 'asking' the muscle to release
- If you have had an injury, massage above and below the point of pain rather directly over where it is sore

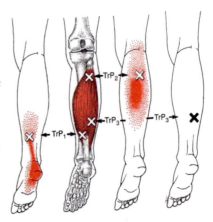

Soleus Stretch

The Gastrocnemius muscle is targeted in the normal straight leg calf stretch. To stretch the Soleus muscle, we need to bring the foot in closer and bend the knee. This releases the stretch on the Gastrocnemious and allows you to get deeper into the calf. Please note that some people with very flexible ankles may not feel this stretch. This is Ok! Just focus on the other stretches.

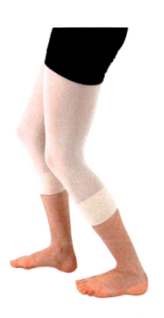

1. Start in the same position as for a Gastrocnemius Stretch, but bring the back foot in so that the big toe is in line with the opposite heel.

2. Bend both knees, until you feel a stretch lower in the calf of the back leg. Keep both heels on the floor, with your toes pointing straight ahead of you.

3. Focus on consciously relaxing the muscle to move deeper into the stretch. Do three repetitions of 30 second holds on each leg, alternating legs after each one.

Note:
- Make sure that both feet are facing forward in parallel
- You should not feel any pinching or pain at the front of the ankle. If you do, avoid this stretch and try the Flexor Digitorum Stretch instead
- Also - focus on relaxing the tendons at the front when you are in first position, and try the "Mid Foot Mobility" exercise in the front of the book, or massage into the arch.
- Keep your body upright and your tummy muscles on

Notes:

Achilles Tendon

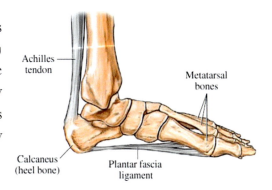

Both the Gastrocnemius and the Soleus muscles attach into the Achilles Tendon, a strong thick tendon that connects these two large calf muscles into the heel bone (Calcaneus). Many dancers say that they have problems with their Achilles Tendon, but it is often a poorly understood, and very commonly misdiagnosed injury.

There are many other causes for pain at the back of the ankle, so do not assume that you have a problem with your Achilles by pain alone. Other things that may give you pain behind the ankle include an extra bone at the back of the ankle called an Os Trigonum, or a syndrome know as Posterior Impingement. If you have injured your Achilles Tendon, it will often be tender with a gentle squeeze of the tendon. If you have pain in this area, check with a sports doctor or physiotherapist to get a correct diagnosis before you do any rehabilitation exercises.

Achilles issues respond best if treatment is started at an early stage. Long-standing Achilles Tendonopathy may require an intense rehabilitation program of up to six months. This is because it has usually developed over a long period of time, and is usually due to weaknesses or imbalances in several different areas, so it is important to correct all of these to gain a full recovery.

The keys to successful rehabilitation of Achilles Tendonopathy are:
- Early diagnosis and avoiding aggravating activities to prevent further damage
- An Eccentric Calf Strengthening Program (described later in this section)
- Correction of any predisposing factors such as muscle tightness, weakness or abnormal movement patterns
- Appropriate progression to functional activities and dance specific rehabilitation
- Massage and mobilisation of the foot may also be required

Check Your Heel Position!

Having the heel bone (Calcaneus) in a good position is essential to settling any pain in the back of the ankle. Get your partner to check the alignment of the heel in several different positions. Some dancers may require a special crafted orthotic to wear in their school and sport shoes, however as you cannot wear these devices in your ballet shoes or pointe shoes it is important that you can control your heel position yourself.

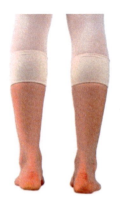 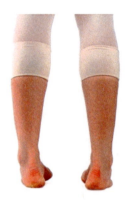 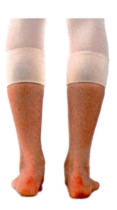

1. Stand in bare feet facing away from your partner. Turn your thigh bones in and out, noticing the difference that this makes to the position of your mid foot and heel bone.

2. Roll the heel bone in and out feeling, for your full range of motion, then feel the centre of your heel pressing down into the floor. Get your partner to check the alignment of your heel bone. Making sure that the Achilles Tendon is vertical

3. Make sure that you have equal weight through both your big toe and the little toe joints. Keep 60% of your weight on the ball of the foot and 40% on the heel. Do this by preparing to rise, rather than by leaning forward.

Note:
- Take note of the tendons at the front of the ankle and see if you can keep them relaxed

Eccentric Rises

One of the most effective ways to strengthen and lengthen the Achilles Tendon is by performing Eccentric Rises. "Eccentric exercises" are exercises where the muscle is contracting while it is lengthening. This sounds odd, but it is possible!

While these exercises are often the best option for rehabilitating Achilles problems, they do have the potential to cause damage if performed inappropriately or excessively. Make sure that you get a diagnosis from a qualified medical professional before doing these exercises if you have any pain. If you do not have pain however, they can be a great way to prevent it!

You should always perform the exercise cautiously. It is normal to get a small amount of discomfort when you begin the strengthening program and at each new load. You should only progress to the next exercise when the previous level is pain-free both during and following the activity. Always ice the tendon after these exercises, keeping it in a lengthened position. If you do not have any available steps to perform this exercise off, you may place the balls of your feet on top of a sturdy book.

Stage One – Double Leg Heel Drop

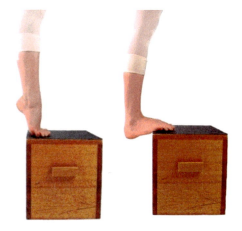

1. Start with both feet on the edge of a step in parallel, pelvis in neutral. Place one foot and then the other onto demi-pointe without actually rising.
2. Straighten the knees then slowly lower your heels to below the level of the step for a count of 3.
3. Place them back on demi-pointe one at a time, and repeat 10 times.
4. If there is a lot of pain in one ankle, take more load through the non-painful side initially.

Stage Two – Increase Load

1. Slowly begin to increase the amount of body weight through the injured leg.
2. Make sure that the feet stay in good alignment.
3. Repeat for two sets of 15, twice a day.

Stage Three - Single Leg Heel Drop

1. Rise using both feet to demi pointe, then transfer your weight to one foot.
2. Slowly lower on one leg, keeping the heel bone vertical and arches gently activated.
3. Repeat for three sets of 15, twice a day. Progress to three times a day.

Stage Four – Increase Speed

1. Start as for the single leg heel drop, with a slow rise on two feet. Transfer to one foot, and then lower the heel quickly to below the level of the step.
2. Progress to adding weight, especially if you are very light. Try using leg weights or a back pack on the front of your body containing bags of sugar/books etc).

Note:
- Always ice the area (on a stretch) after doing the exercises, ideally in an ice bath, to settle any inflammation

Achilles Tendon Massage

Many people who experience pain in the Achilles want to rub it, or massage it. I actually advise against this. The pain that you may get in the Achilles tendon is often actually degeneration rather than inflammation, and rubbing it can make it a lot worse rather than better!

Any hands-on treatment to assist the rehabilitation of an Achilles Tendonopathy should be focused on the areas above and below the pain. It is much better to massage the Gastrocnemius, Soleus, and the other deeper calf muscles or the foot to reduce the load on the Achilles, rather than massaging where it is sore. Rubbing over the area of pain can actually irritate it further so please do not do this!

Note:
- Always get a medical professional to officially diagnose any pain at the back of the ankle before you start any of these exercises
- Any Achilles Tendon rehabilitation must be combined with core, pelvic stability and flexibility work
- Also make sure to review the Intrinsic Foot Exercises towards the end of this book

Notes:

The Peroneals

The Peroneals are the group of muscles that run down the outside of the lower leg and attach via tendons down onto the outside of the foot. They are obviously involved in maintaining alignment of the ankle, and this is especially important en pointe. Effective use of the Peroneals helps counter the "Sickling in" often seen in young dancers.

The Peroneals may also get overused if you overly "Fish" the foot for aesthetics en l'air. Some companies and choreographers prefer the line that this gives, however it is important that this position is not maintained when the foot becomes the supporting foot. Fishing en pointe puts huge strain through the inner arch of the foot and can result in serious injury to the foot, ankle or knee.

Peroneus Longus

Origin:
The biggest of the three peroneal muscles attaches to the upper portion of the Fibula, just below the outside of the knee.

Insertion:
It attaches into the foot via a long tendon that curves behind the ankle bone and then under the outside of the foot before attaching onto the base of the first metatarsal and medial cuneiform bones.

Action:
Peroneus Longus points and everts (fishes) the foot, and helps stabilise the outside of the ankle. Overuse of this muscle can result in pain on the outside of the leg or ankle.

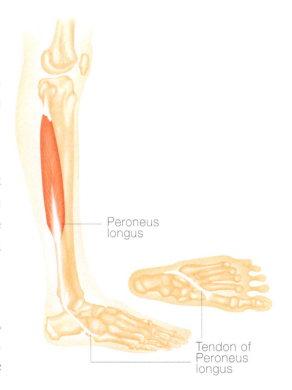

Peroneus Brevis

Origin:
The Peroneus Brevis arises from the bottom half of the Fibula.

Insertion:
Its tendon passes behind the ankle bone to insert on the base of the fifth metatarsal. It is interesting to note that some people have a much longer tendonous portion of this muscle than others.

Action:
The Peroneus Brevis points and everts (fishes) the foot.

Peroneus Tertius (Not Always Present):

Origin:
The bottom 1/3 of the front of the fibula.

Insertion:
The top surface of the base of the 5th metatarsal.

Action:
Flexes and everts the foot at the ankle.

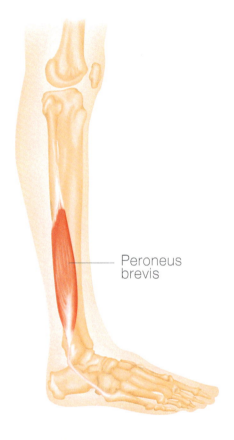

Peroneus brevis

Peroneus Quartus (Rarely Present):

Some people may even have a 4th peroneal muscle! This is often only discovered if the dancer has an ultrasound or an MRI to investigate an injury. Peroneus Quartus (when present) is a tiny muscle that has no real known function.

Pointe through the Demi-Pointe with Resistance Band

This is a good way to strengthen the Peroneal muscles throughout their full range, as needed by a dancer. Make sure to keep the ankle aligned at all times.

1. Sit on the floor with your legs outstretched with a pillow or small ball between your knees and the spine straight. Place a resistance band around the outside of your left ankle. Hold both ends of the band in your right hand and place the right foot over the band so that the band is now pulling the left foot in. Focus on using the muscles up the side of your lower leg to bring the ankle back into alignment.

2. Slowly pointe the left ankle, keeping the toes pulled back, maintaining the alignment of the ankle. Hold the ankle stable while you point the toes, keeping the middle joints of the toes long.

3. Slowly flex the toes, and then the ankle. Repeat 10 – 20 times, on each side. The peroneals will start get warm as they fatigue.

Note:
- Keep sitting up nice and tall during this exercise, with your spine in neutral – if this is difficult due to tight hamstrings, try sitting on a folded towel or small cushion
- If your Peroneal muscles are already tight, it may be better to start with the massage techniques and progress to the strengthening once the muscles are more relaxed

Resistance Band Rises with Transfers

This is a good way to strengthen the Peroneal muscles in the range that they are needed for pointe work, especially if you tend to sickle en pointe. Many girls do not use their full height of rise when working on demi-pointe, and then 'snap' into their full range en pointe. This results in irritation and stretching of the ligaments at the front of the ankle, or compression in the back of the ankle and is obviously best avoided! Make sure that you always perform a few of the double leg variations before you progress to the single leg versions.

Variation 1

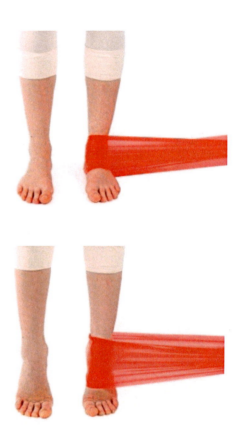

1. Place a resistance band around the inside of one ankle and tie the ends together around a table leg. Make sure that the band is spread out over the heel, not straight over the Achilles tendon.

2. Slowly rise onto demi-pointe, keeping your weight centred and the ankles straight. The band will be pulling the ankle into a sickled position so take care to maintain your alignment, with your weight between your first and second toes. Feel the muscles up the outside of the ankle working to keep it in line.

3. Slowly lower the heels, keeping your arches on, and your toes long.

4. Do 5 - 10 rises in this position.

Variation 2

1. To make this exercise a little more challenging, rise in parallel, pushing up to your full height of rise. Make sure to keep your feet and ankles aligned.

2. Slowly transfer your weight over onto the foot with the band around it, maintaining your full height of rise and alignment of the ankle. You may find that the heel drops a little, but work towards being able to maintain your full height of rise.

3. Pause momentarily at the full height of rise, making sure that your hips are level, and your shoulders relaxed, and then slowly lower the heel, keeping your arches activated. Repeat 10 times on each side, rising with two feet and lowering on one.

Variation 3

1. Keep the foot with the band attached pointing to the barre, and turn your body a quarter turn to place the feet in first position. Your body will now be almost side on to the barre, and the band should be placed directly back behind your ankle.

2. Slowly rise onto demi-pointe, keeping your weight centred and the ankles straight. Feel your turnout muscles at the top of the hip working to keep the leg in line.

3. Slowly lower the heels into first position, keeping your arches on and your toes long. Repeat 10 times.

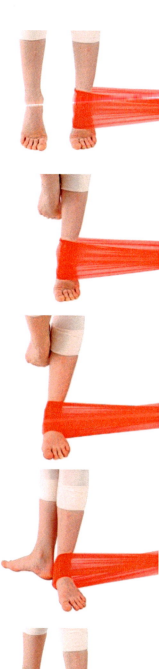
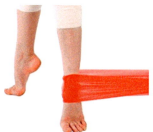

Variation 4

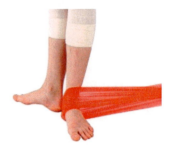

1. Start in first position, with the band pulling directly back behind you. You do not need very much tension in the band, as this exercises is more difficult than it looks!

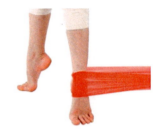

2. Slowly rises in turnout, maintaining your placement by using the deep rotators of the hips. Make sure that you are correctly placed on demi-pointe, with weight down through your second toe, rather than over your big or little toes.

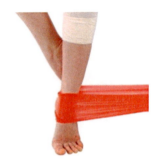

3. Slowly transfer your weight over onto to the foot with the band around it, maintaining your full height of rise, controlling the turnout of your supporting leg and keeping your hips square to the front. Hold the full height of rise for a count of three keeping the toes long.

4. Slowly lower the heel to the floor, aiming to finish with the foot in exactly the same position that you started in! This is a very challenging exercise so please make sure you have mastered the other variations first!

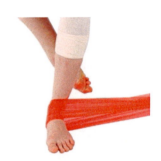

Note:
- Keep your weight between the 1st and 2nd toes
- Keep your toes long and flat to the floor
- Keep the muscles in the arch of the foot activated as you lower your heel
- Make sure that your heel lands in the same place it started at when lowering from each rise

Peroneal Massage

The Peroneals may get overused if you overly "Fish" the foot for aesthetics en l'air. Tension in the Peroneals can cause quite a bit of pain in the outer part of the lower leg, and may even block your range in a developpé devant by restricting the sliding of the nerves down the outer part of the lower leg.

1. Sit with the left leg turned in and the right leg turned out, with both knees bent. Apply some massage cream to the outer part of the leg. Lean back on your right hand or elbow to get the right angle of force.

2. Slowly massage up the outside of the shin in long slow strokes, using your Pisiform bone – on the outer border of the heel of your hand. You may also try using your knuckles to massage this area if this feels easier.

3. Spend 2–5 minutes on each leg. Massage a maximum of every 2 days on the same area.

4. Try holding sustained pressure on the trigger points indicated in the picture off to the left.

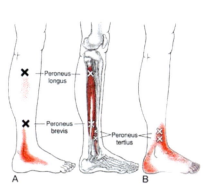

Note:
- You can use any kind of massage cream to do this massage, but if there is any soreness try using a natural anti-inflammatory cream for extra effect
- Remember to do this prior to strengthening if you are tight in this area

Peroneal Stretches

Some people will feel this stretch and some people won't. It depends on the flexibility of the ankle joints and just how tight the muscles are. If you don't feel it, don't worry! It simply means that this is not an area that you need to focus on. Focus on the massage or other areas instead.

Peroneus Longus and Peroneus Brevis

1. Start as for a regular calf stretch, facing the barre, with one foot forward, and one foot back with the leg straight. Then roll onto the outside of the back foot, so that the shin bone is twisting out slightly. This should give a gentle stretch up the outside and back of the lower leg.
2. You can either stay in this stretch for a few seconds, or move slowly in and out of the stretch.

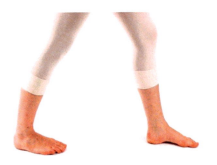

Peroneus Tertius

1. In standing or sitting, tuck the foot under to stretch the front and side of the ankle.
2. Avoid this stretch if you are already very mobile through the front of the ankle.

Note:
- If you don't feel one or both of these stretches don't worry!
- Go gently with any stretches around the ankle, there should be no pain with either of these stretches

Notes:

Tibialis Anterior

Tibialis Anterior (TA) is a muscle that has its muscle belly on the front of the shin bone and has a tendon that attaches down to the inner arch and underneath surface of the foot. (Tibialis = of the shin bone, Anterior = front) Due to its position, the obvious action of Tibialis Anterior is to actively flex (dorsiflex) and while this action may seem infrequent in classical ballet, many dancers have problems with the Tibialis Anterior due to overuse.

The Tibialis Anterior (TA) has a strong fascial band around it which means that if the muscle swells a lot of pressure can build inside the compartment and result in a lot of pain. This issue is called Anterior Compartment Syndrome. Two other injuries called Medial Tibial Stress Syndrome (MTSS) and Tibial Stress Fracture also occur due to overuse of the muscle. All of these issues are often lumped together under the poorly identified diagnosis of 'Shin Splints'.

The TA will also get very tight if a dancer attempts to correct her foot position by lifting the arches with this muscle instead of using the muscles under the foot to support the position of the arch from underneath.

Tibialis Anterior

Origin:
Upper 2/3 of the shin bone (Tibia) and the membrane that sits between the two bones of the lower leg (Interosseous Membrane).

Insertion:
Underneath the Medial Cuneiform and First Metatarsal bone.

Action:
Flexes the ankle and turns the foot in (inversion). It also assists in supporting the medial longitudinal arch of foot.

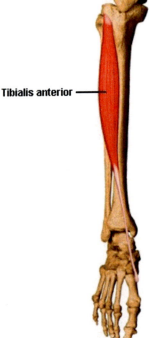

Weight-Bearing Awareness

If a dancer constantly has her weight back on her heels the Tibialis Anterior will be constantly switched on and will become very tight and thickened. In addition, often the TA will try to pull the shin forward when going into a plié or en fondu, which can cause further tension to build and restrict plié range. This simple issue with weight placement can be the source of many foot issues that plague keen dancers.

1. Stand with your feet in parallel. Find a position where you can feel equal weight under the big and little toe joints, and slightly more pressure on the ball of the foot than the heel. We call this position "Tripod Foot".
2. Make sure that the arches are gently activated, without rolling your weight too far onto the outer part of the foot. Relax the tendons at the front of the ankle, and hold this position for 10 seconds.
3. Try closing your eyes and see how much more aware you are of what is going on in the feet! You may feel a little unstable at first, but this really helps develop your awareness and balance!
4. Repeat with the feet in first position and if possible, get a friend to check if the tendons at the front of the ankle are relaxed and your arches are supported. Try not to look at your own feet!

Note:
- Feel like you are almost rising, rather than leaning forward, in order to keep the tendon at the front of the ankle relaxed
- Ask a friend to watch, or use a mirror to check if the tendons are relaxed, rather than looking down, as this will make them switch on!

Tibialis Anterior Strengthening

While it may be very tight, the Tibialis Anterior may also be weak, so rehabilitation may need to involve specific strengthening as well as awareness exercises to functionally release it. Many people forget that it is important for this muscle to be strong. Strengthening the front of the shin may also help release tension in the deep calf muscles (Reciprocal Inhibition.)

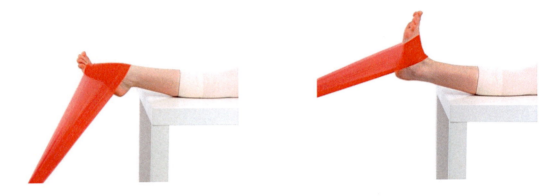

1. Sit on a chair with one leg outstretched, supported on another chair, keeping the spine straight. Place a resistance band around the front of your ankle. Have a partner hold both ends of the band down to the floor, or attach them to a sturdy leg of a table. You may like to put a few pillows under your calf for comfort.

2. Slowly pull the foot back against the resistance of the band, feeling a gentle contraction through the front of the shin. If you feel any cramping in this muscle, it is an indication that the muscle is very weak. Reduce the tension on the band and do only small repetitions until it begins to feel more comfortable.

3. Aim for 20 slow repetitions against a medium resistance.

Note:
- Some people may find this very easy to do. If it is very easy, this just means that it's not an important one for you to do!

Self Massage - Tibialis Anterior

Massaging out the tension that is in the Tibialis Anterior is important in the rehabilitation of any shin pain to reduce the pulling of the muscle on the surface of the shin bone. However, learning how to use the foot correctly is also essential to avoid the tension from building up again.

1. Try massaging up the length of the muscle in long strokes to help relax the strong fibrous covering that is around the muscle. Then try some short, slow, strong stokes as if to pull the muscle sideways, away from the shin bone.

2. Make sure that you do not let the joints in your fingers overextend when you do the massage. Try using different parts of your hand, your knuckles or your opposite heel for variety.

3. Even better, try and swap massages with a friend or parent! If you have a partner that can help you, they can do a long slow movement as you point your foot, to release the fascia even quicker.

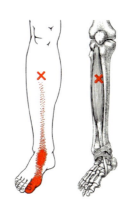

Note:
- If your shins feel great after being massaged out, then you definitely need to work out why the tension is there in the first place
- Go back to the weight bearing awareness exercise and make sure that you can stand in parallel, first and fifth positions with the tendon at the front of the ankle relaxed

Tibialis Anterior Stretch

Many people will be fine with just the massage for the front of the shin, and will not feel this stretch. However, if you are very tight in the front of the ankle, you may like to try stretching the muscle a little. You can try the "Pointe Stretch" that is in "The Perfect Pointe Book" or this stretch in standing.

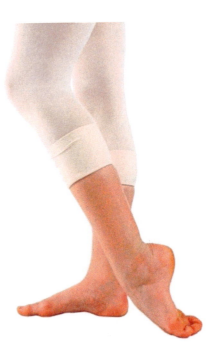

1. Start by standing in parallel. Bend one knee and lift the foot off the floor, before tucking the front part of the foot under.

2. Gently press forward into the front of the foot until you feel a gentle stretch in the front of the ankle and up into the shin.

3. Try rolling the foot out and in to target different parts of the muscle.

4. If you already have a very mobile open ankle, you do not need to do this stretch. Make sure that there is no discomfort in the back or the front of the ankle.

Note:
- Only do this stretch if you are very tight through the front of the ankle
- If you have very mobile ankles, overstretching them can cause instability
- You should feel no pain at the front or the back of the ankle during this stretch

Notes:

Tibialis Posterior

Tibialis Posterior – as described by its name - is a muscle that sits on the back (Posterior) of the shin bone (Tibia). This muscle really helps get that little bit of extra height and 'lock off' on demi pointe.

The Tibialis Posterior is the most central of all the deep leg muscles and sits deep in the back of the calf. Many dancers, especially those with not very good range do not use this muscle effectively. It can also be underdeveloped in those dancers that have good pointe range. This is identified when they can demonstrate good range when rising on two legs, but struggle to achieve this range on a single leg or en pointe.

Tibialis Posterior is essential in keeping the ankle pointed when lowering slowly from full pointe onto demi-pointe.

Learning how to activate this muscle properly can actually help improve your pointe range over time, especially if you feel blocked in the back of the ankle when you point your foot.

Tibialis Posterior

Origin:
Inner posterior borders of the Tibia and Fibula.

Insertion:
The tendon passes under the medial maleolus and then splits into three parts, attaching to the bases of the 2nd, 3rd and 4th metatarsals, the 1st, 2nd and 3rd cuniforms, the cuboid, the navicular and the Calcaneus.

Action:
Tibialis Posterior is the key muscle for stabilisation of the ankle on demi-pointe and full pointe, but can also sickle the ankle.

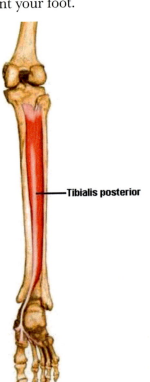

Seated Rises

To get an awareness of the placement and function of the Tibialis Posterior, we need to go back to an exercise that we did in "The Perfect Pointe Book" but with a slightly different focus.

1. Start in sitting with the feet in parallel, with the heel slightly further back than the knees. Slowly push one foot up onto demi pointe. Have an awareness of pulling up from just in front of the heel to deep up into the back of the calf, to take the foot to its full height of demi pointe.

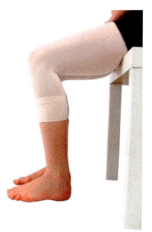

2. To test that you are actually using the Tibialis Posterior, see if you can relax the big calf muscles while maintaining the full height of demi pointe. This may take a little practice, especially if you do not have very flexible ankles.

3. Slowly lower the heel, seeing if you can feel the skin of the sole of the foot staying up off the floor. Repeat 10 times, then repeat with the foot and leg turned out.

Note:
- Keep the spine upright when doing the seated rises
- Make sure to check that the big calf muscle can relax at the height of rise
- Keep the toes long and relaxed, and the ankle in good alignment throughout

Rises in First Position

Once you have an awareness of how your Tibialis Posterior functions, you want to get an awareness of how it works when you are dancing. A good way to practice this is simply to practice double leg rises in first position at the barre, with a slightly different focus than you normally do. Learning how to control the Tibialis Posterior when en pointe really helps you 'lift up' out of your pointe shoes.

1. Start by facing the barre in parallel and then slowly rise in parallel. Feel an extra lift from just in front of your heel, pushing you right up onto your full height of demi-pointe. Please note that when doing these rises your big calf muscles are meant to come on! (The isolation exercise that we did previously is just to check that the Tibialis Posterior is active).

2. Slowly lower the heels maintaining control of the arches. Repeat 10 times.

3. Repeat the exercise in first position, focusing on using the Tibilalis Posterior to get an extra lift at the end of range. Remember to keep using your turnout muscles so that you lower your heels back into first position without wiggling into place!

Note:
- Focus on working through the foot, as though you are peeling it off the floor
- Make sure to control the ankles carefully to avoid 'snapping' into your end range

Tibialis Posterior Massage

If you have never really used this muscle before often it is quite stiff and lacking in blood flow. Massage can help wake up the muscle and release any deep tension that is preventing it from functioning correctly. Go gently when you are massaging muscles this deep, and remember that you shouldn't be sore afterwards.

1. Sit with the right leg turned in and the left leg turned out, with both knees bent. Apply a small amount of massage cream to the middle of your Gastrocnemius muscle.

2. To find your Tibialis Posterior you will need to feel deep between the two parts of Gastrocnemius close to the bone. Do some small slow sustained deep releases drawing up through the muscle, only moving about an inch or two at a time.

3. Try some trigger point releases on the tighter, more tender points of this muscle by breathing in and out using your mind to release the tension in the muscle, rather than just rubbing it.

4. Follow the trigger point releases with some gentle strokes along the whole calf.

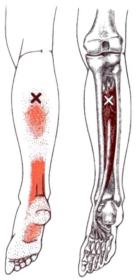

Note:
- If you have been working your Tibialis Posterior a lot it may be a little tender at first
- Remember to go gently with very small scooping movements or trigger point releases

Tibialis Posterior Stretch

Some people don't feel much when stretching their Soleus muscle so this is a nice way to release the muscles deep into the calf. This technique is very similar to the massage but gives a stretch by gliding the muscle under your fingers.

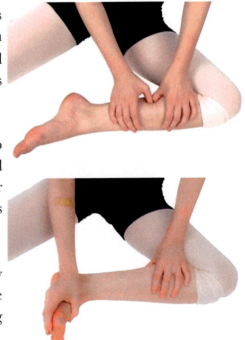

1. Go into the same position as you did with the Tibialis Posterior massage, with one leg bent in front of you and the other tucked in behind. With one hand find the Tibialis posterior muscle (between the two heads of gastrocnemius) and apply slight pressure onto it.

2. Maintaining that pressure, use your other hand to slowly flex your foot back so the muscle is stretched out under your fingers. The top hand can either remain still or apply a small glide over the muscle as you flex your foot.

3. Repeat this in different parts of the muscle belly by moving the position of the top hand slightly. Make sure that you do not feel any pain after performing this stretch.

Note:
- It can be nice to retest your Soleus stretch afterwards to see the improvement in range

Notes:

Lumbricals and Interossei

The Intrinsic Foot Muscles are all of the muscles that start and end within the foot. They are designed to stabilize the foot over uneven surfaces and help us balance. The layout of the muscles and bones in our feet is very similar to the structure of our hands. While all of the intrinsic foot muscles are important to the dancer, several are essential to master. Common issues resulting from poor intrinsic foot control include the formation of bunions, blisters, deformed toes and overuse of the extrinsic foot muscles

The Lumbricals sit in between each of the toes in the ball of the foot and help flex the joint between the long toe bones (metatarsals) and the actual toes (phalanges).

Together with Flexor Hallucis Brevis and Flexor Digitorum Brevis they are essential in learning how to point the toes from the metatarsophalangeal joints (where the toes join into the foot). Correct use of these muscles is essential in avoiding overloading of the Flexor Digitorum Longis which can be identified by feeling in the back of the calf and scrunching the toes when pointing the foot.

Keeping the toes long using these muscles is also the best way to avoid blisters on the knuckles when en pointe as this occurs when the flexed toes rub on the canvas of the inside of the shoe. There are some other tiny foot muscles called your Interossei that lie either side of each of your toes. While there are four Dorsal Interossei on the top of the foot, there are only three Plantar Interossei, which means that often the second toe is harder to control than the others when pointing the toes.

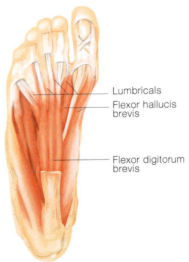

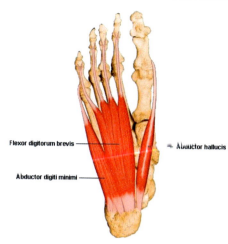

Abducens Hallucis sits on the outside of the big toe and is very important in controlling the alignment of the big toe and reducing the development of bunions in susceptible individuals. This is quite a hard muscle for many people to find, and often we have to use electrical stimulation to wake it up!

Abductor Digiti Minimi is a tiny muscle that helps control the little toe. For some people this works well naturally, but others will need to train it more.

All of these Intrinsic Foot Muscles help support the Plantar Fascia in its role of propelling the foot off the floor in gait and in petit allegro. Weakness in these muscles can result in collapsing of the arch, overload of the plantar fascia, plantar fasciitis and development of a heel spur.

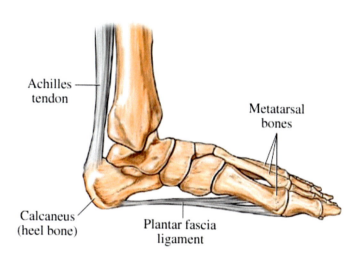

Doming

This exercise takes time to master, but is essential to be able to pointe your toes properly and to keep them long in your pointe shoes, preventing a lot of blisters! This exercise works the Lumbricals and Flexor Digitorum Brevis muscles

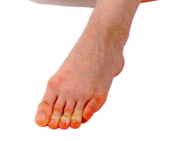

1. Sit on a chair or the floor with the feet in parallel. Keeping the pads of the toes on the floor, feel like you are creating a dome shaped space under the knuckles, as if you could hide something under the ball of your foot.

2. Keep the toes long, and maintain a gentle pressure through the tips of the toes and the centre of the heel. If the toes keep curling under, try stretching out the undersurface of the toes against a wall, or massaging the undersurface of the foot. If the muscles are too tight it will be hard to get them to work correctly.

3. Repeat slowly 20 times on each foot, keeping the middle of the foot aligned at all times. If you are having trouble with finding the right muscles to use, place your hand beside your foot and perform the exercise with your hand at the same time. Because you have very similar muscles and bones in your hands compared to your feet, and you are used to using these muscles, this can help a lot!

Note:
- In the beginning the tendon at the front of the ankle will come on when you do this exercise. This is ok
- As you get better you can try to keep this tendon relaxed to really refine the exercise

Toe Swapping

This is a great way to train the small muscles that help to control the toes when dancing, and is really helpful when progressing onto pointe. This will take time to perfect! While it may feel impossible at first, the control of these muscles will improve with regular practise. It is simply a matter of learning how to tell the nerves that control these muscles what to do!

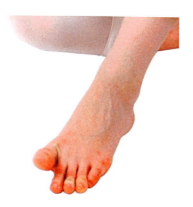 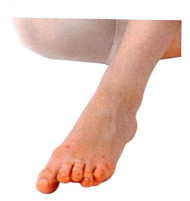

1. Sit on a chair with feet in parallel, and place feet in the 'Tripod Foot' position with the centre of the heel grounded and equal pressure through your big toe joint and your little toe joint. Make sure the inner arch and under surface of your foot is active. Slowly lift the big toe off the floor keeping all the small toes down.
2. Next, lower the big toe and raise all the other little toes off the floor. Make sure that the arches of the feet stay on, and that the foot does not twist or roll from side to side.
3. Continue swapping between the big and little toes at least 20 times. The ball of the foot must stay in contact with the floor at all times. You can use your fingers to help isolate the movement initially.

Note:
- Initially you may find your arch wants to roll in and out as you lift your toes. Doing this will work your extrinsic muscles deep in your calf rather than your smaller intrinsic foot muscles
- Make sure the foot stays centred with your arch lifted as you swap your toes

Piano Playing

This exercise will definitely take time to perfect, but it will help improve the control of your toes a lot. Being able to really articulate all of your toes helps your balance enormously, and gives a lovely shape to the front of the foot. Try testing the rest of your family and see if any of them can do these exercises!

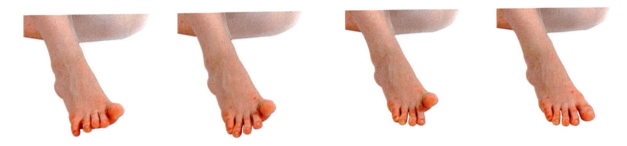

1. Set your feet up as for toe swapping. Keep the centre of your heel and the ball the foot flat on the floor throughout the exercise. To start, lift all of the toes off the floor keeping the ball of the foot on the floor.

2. Place the toes back down on the floor, one by one, starting with your pinkie (little toe). Make sure that the arches of the feet stay on, and that the foot does not roll from side to side.

3. Reverse the exercise, by lifting up the big toe, then the other toes, one by one, very slowly. It is often hard to separate the second and third toes, but keep working at it and you will be surprised how good you will get!

Note:
- You can use your hands to assist the placement of your toes in the beginning
- Make sure not to roll the foot as you place each toe down

Intrinsic Foot Massage

The small muscles on the top of the foot (Extensor Digitorum Brevis) and in between the toes (Dorsal Interossei) are very tight in some people. If you notice that your toes tend to sit in a bent position even when relaxed this may be a good exercise for you. This is also good if you find it very hard to pointe your toes from the knuckles, or do the doming exercise. If the fibrous tissue on the top of the foot is too tight, it will be very hard to point the foot properly.

1. Place a small amount of massage cream on the top of the foot. Feel for the space between your big toe bone (Hallux) and your second toe bone (Second Metatarsal) with the index finger of one hand. Some people like to add extra pressure by placing the index finger of the other hand on top.

2. Slowly massage between the two toe bones, drawing from the web space between the toes up into the middle of the foot. Do the same for each space along the top of the foot (Four lines in total).

3. There will often be small sharp points of tension. Work on these gently over time and you will see good results.

Note:
- Make sure to avoid any areas of sharp, shooting pain as these are usually small nerves!
- Try pointing your foot again after you have finished massaging it to test for any increase in range

Intrinsic Foot Stretch

After massaging out the front of the foot, it is nice to give it a gentle stretch. This stretch actually works on the fascia that covers the front of the foot as well as any tight muscles. Again, some people will not feel this stretch at all, which simply means that they don't really need to do it. Others will feel it very strongly and will find it of great benefit. Remember to always take any new stretches slowly and carefully. They should not be painful!

1. Start in standing, or sitting on a chair. Tuck the toes of one foot underneath and gently press into the floor to stretch across the top of the knuckles. Each of the knuckle bones should show.

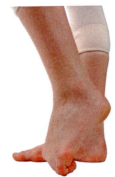

2. Hold for a few seconds then place the foot into a demi-pointe position to release the stretch.

3. You shouldn't feel any pain when you are doing this, but you may feel a strong stretch through the front of your foot if it is very tight.

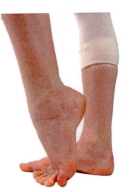

4. After releasing the tension in the top of the foot, try pointing your foot, keeping the toes long and bending from these knuckles to feel the difference.

Note:
- If you don't feel a stretch, don't worry! If you can see all of your knuckle bones then you are already free enough in this area
- If the stretch is very strong, try doing it after a shower when you are warm

Notes:

Flexor Hallucis Longus (FHL)

Flexor Hallucis Longus is an extrinsic foot muscle that has a long tendon all the way down to the tip of the big toe. (Flexor = To bend, Hallucis = The Big Toe, Longus = Long).

The FHL is one of the muscles that is most commonly operated on in the student dancer and is chronically overused in many individuals. If the big toe (Hallux) is "Hooked" when pointing the foot, this indicates the the FHL is being used too much and this may lead to thickening and irritation of the FHL Tendon. This is sometimes called 'Trigger Toe' as if the thickened portion of tendon gets restricted at the back of the ankle, the big toe may get stuck in flexion!

Several other issues may contribute to the development of FHL problems, especially poor control of the Flexor Hallucis Brevis (FHB) muscle, instability in the ankle joint and rolling in of the medial arch. Often supportive orthotics can help to control the position of the foot, however as Orthotics may not be worn in ballet shoes, appropriate strengthening of the appropriate muscles to control the foot is essential.

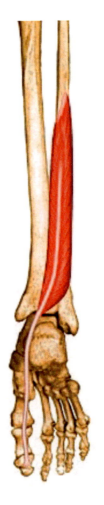

Origin:
The middle section of the shaft of the Fibula and the Interosseous Membrane. (While in some pictures the FHL looks like it is on the inside of the ankle, in reality the muscle belly sits more on the outside of the leg, just to the side of the Achilles tendon.)

Insertion:
The FHL tendon passes under the Achilles Tendon, around the inside of the heel bone and then goes all of the way down to the end of the big toe.

Action:
Pointes and sickles the foot; flexes the big toe at all joints, and is the 'push off' muscle during walking. Many dancers over use this muscle causing irritation in the tendon.

Flexor Hallucis Brevis (FHB)

Flexor Hallucis Brevis is a very important muscle for any dancer. When working well it assists with rising onto pointe, creating a beautiful line to the front of the foot, pushing off in jumps and controlling the position of the foot en fondu.

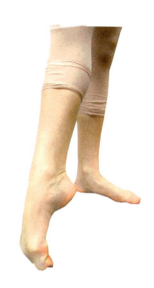

However, if the FHB is not working effectively FHL overworks and this can lead to all kinds of problems such as rolling in of the arches and hooking of the big toe, and can therefore contribute to the development of injuries such as FHL Tendonopathy, Achilles Tendonopathy and may other foot problems.

Unfortunately, many people are completely unaware of this muscle and do not know how to strengthen it effectively. The good thing is that a few simple exercises can make a very big difference to your dancing!

Origin:
The Flexor Hallucis Brevis attaches to the medial part of the under surface of the Cuboid, under the third Cuneiform and the tendon of the Tibialis Posterior.

Insertion:
The FHB divides into two parts and attaches into the medial and lateral sides of the base of the big toe, with a sesamoid bone in each tendon. The sessamoid bones help create a tunnel for the FHL tendon to travel through.

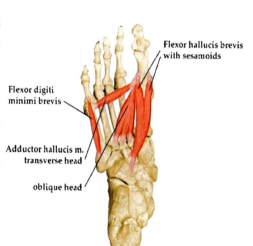

Action:
FHB flexes the big toe at base of the big toe (the MTP joint), and provides support to the front of the medial arch of the foot.

Big Toe Exercise

This is a great way to learn how to use the small muscle that sits under the big toe (Flexor Hallucis Brevis (FHB). It is important that this muscle is strong to support the front of the arch, to push off in jumps, and to rise smoothly from demi-pointe onto full pointe. A strong FHB will also help take the load off your FHL.

1. Kneel on one knee with the other foot placed flat on the floor. Make sure that the weight is distributed evenly throughout the foot, with equal weight under your big and little toe joints. Lift the big toe off the floor, keeping all of the little toes down.

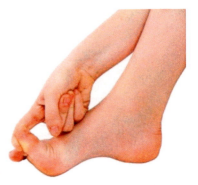

2. Using the muscle under the big toe push the big toe down towards the floor, keeping the middle joint of the big toe straight, against the resistance of your thumb, and hold for 3 seconds. Make sure that the arches of the feet stay on, the middle joint of the big toe stays straight and that the foot does not twist. Slowly relax the contraction, and pull the toe back up. Repeat at least 20 times.

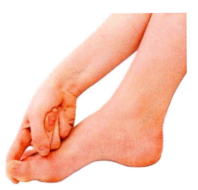

3. Next, see if you can press the pad of the big toe down into the floor in standing, using the FHB muscle. This should help shape the front part of your medial arch. Hold for a few seconds and release. This should be a subtle contraction and the front of your ankle should stay relaxed.

Note:
- The FHB can also help you balance!
- When standing on one leg if the pressure rolls onto the inside of your foot you can actually use the big toe to help stabilise the front of the foot so you don't topple over

Tendus en Croix

Being able to correctly perform a Tendu is one of the most important skills in classical ballet, from both a technique perspective and for injury prevention. Pay close attention to how you work the foot on the floor, making sure to work through the demi-pointe position before stretching the toes. It is important to practice this without your shoes on as it is amazing what you can hide inside a pair of ballet flats, and even more in a pair of demi-pointe shoes.

Tendu Devant

1. Stand in 5th with the right foot front, and your hands on your hips.

2. Slowly push the foot forward into a tendu, lengthening through the front of the ankle to fully pointe the ankle with the toes relaxed. Keep both legs pulled up and turned out.

3. Slowly pointe the toes as though doing the doming exercise, keeping the middle joints of the toes straight. Make sure to fully pointe the toes but no clawing!

4. Return the foot to fifth position, working through the demi-pointe position.

5. Do four slow tendu devant with the right foot, working through the demi-pointe, making sure to fully pointe the ankle before pointing the toes with each one.

6. Then do eight faster tendu, smoothing out the demi-pointe transition, yet still articulating the area fully.

Tendu à la Seconde

1. When performing tendus to second try to integrate the doming exercise. First tendu the foot to the demi-pointe position keeping hips level and square to the front.

2. Work gently against the floor to push up to a fully pointed position keeping the toes long. Make sure that there is no pressure on your big toe and that both hips remain turned out. Make sure to work though the demi-pointe position to close in 5th. Do four slow tendu and then eight fast.

Tendu Derrière

1. When performing a tendu derrière work through the demi pointe position but when fully pointed make sure not to have too much pressure on your big toe. It should be just touching the floor and you should be able to keep your big toe joint long.

2. Too much pressure on the big toe can cause a painful bunion to form at the base of the big toe. Keeping the weight on the supporting leg also helps strengthen your core and turnout more!

Note:
- Keep the supporting foot stable, with arches on and weight over the ball of the foot
- Keep both legs turned out from the hips, with hip bones facing the front

Flexor Hallucis Longus Massage

If you have been scrunching your toes and overusing your FHL for a while then it is nice to give it a release with some massage. Remember that the muscle belly for the FHL about half way between the back of the ankle where your Achilles Tendon is and the outside of the leg where your Peroneal muscles are.

1. Sit on the floor with your left leg turned in and right leg turned out. The foot to be massaged can be pointed or flexed. Apply a small amount of cream onto the outside of your ankle.

2. The FHL muscle sits deep to the Achilles tendon, so you will have to massage carefully in between this tendon and the muscles on the outside of the leg.

3. Use the heel of your hand or your thumb to slowly massage up from the outside of the ankle to half way up your shin.

4. There is no benefit to massaging the FHL tendon, so focus on the muscle belly instead. Spend about two minutes on each leg.

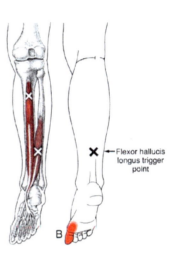

Note:
- People that use their FHL a lot may feel that it is quite thick around this area and it may be tender to touch initially
- Start off very gently. You do not need much pressure to get a good effect. It is amazing how good your ankle can feel afterwards!
- Do not continue if you experience pain in this area

Flexor Hallucis Brevis Massage

We now know that we need to use the little muscle under the big toe (FHB) to point our toes, yet often it is very tight and stiff and hard to get working. Tension in this muscle can also limit your demi-pointe range.

1. In a sitting position, use one hand to gently pull the big toe backwards. Use the other hand to gently massage along the length of the big toe bone from the ball of your foot to the middle of your arch.

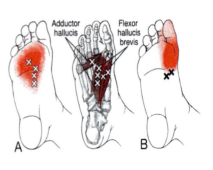

2. A big tendon may pop out as you pull your big toe back. Do not massage directly on this tendon (it is the FHL) but you can gently massage the muscles on either side of it. Use the pictures to find common trigger points in these small foot muscles.

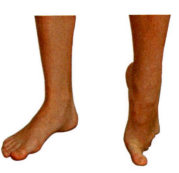

3. After massaging out the tension in this area, try doing a "Split Toe Stretch" to further release tension in the area. After the massage and the stretch, try rising onto demi-pointe and feel the difference these techniques make!

Note:
- You should not feel any pain after doing these massage techniques. Take it gently, and please consult a health professional if you experience any pain

Flexor Hallucis Longus (FHL) Stretch

I no longer promote strong stretching of the FHL tendon. This stretch is one which used to be taught by many therapists, however in the past few years research has suggested that it may not actually be very good for the FHL tendon. One therapist I know manually performed this stretch on a dancer who was undergoing surgery on the FHL tendon (while under anaesthetic) and found that it put a lot of tension through the tendon rather than actually stretching the muscle. If you have not started doing this stretch yet I advise against it. If you have done it in the past, and feel benefit from it please take note of the following tips.

1. Start by placing the under-surface of your big toe against a step and letting your little toes fall to the side. Gently move the foot in close to the step to position the toe in an extended position. If you feel a stretch here, then pause in this position.

2. If no stretch is felt, you may carefully bend your knee forwards. This stretch is ok if you feel it under the big toe or in the FHL muscle belly on the outside of the ankle however if you feel it on the inside of the ankle please do not perform this stretch.

Note:
- Do not continue with this stretch if you feel any pain on the inside of the ankle
- It is better to massage out tension in the muscle belly of FHL than over stretch the tendon

Flexor Digitorum Longus (FDL)

Flexor Digitorum Longus (FDL) is an extrinsic foot muscle that has its muscle belly deep in the back of the calf and has long tendons down into all of the toes. (Flexor = To bend, Digitorum = All the toes, Longus = Long).

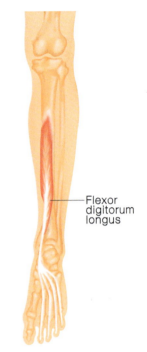

Flexor digitorum longus

Overuse of the Flexor Digitorum Longus is very common in young dancers and is very easy to pick up. If the FDL is working without appropriate intrinsic foot muscle control your toes will 'Claw' under when pointing the foot. This is very important to correct, ideally before any dancer begins pointe work, to avoid overuse injuries to the FDL, pain in the back of the ankle or blisters along the middle joints of the toes.

This can take some time and effort to master, however the massage techniques shown in this course can help make the process much more rapid. Stretches and releases under the toes are often necessary if your toes have been held in a curled position for some time.

Origin:
The back surface of the Tibia.

Insertion:
The tendon runs behind the inner ankle bone and splits into smaller tendons that go to the end bone of each of the small toes.

Action:
FDL assists in pointing the foot and helps the foot grip the ground, especially on uneven surfaces. It also curls the toes under and may make sickle the ankle.

Note:
A lot of the exercises often given to dancers to improve their feet involve picking up items with the toes or bringing things towards you. Unfortunately these exercises encourage scrunching of the toes and over use of FDL. It is important to focus more on keeping the toes long and working the muscles deep in the foot rather than tightening up the muscles deep in the calf.

Pointe Through Demi-Pointe with Ball

This exercise helps you learn how to work the little muscles that control your toes in isolation from the bigger muscles that pointe your ankle. This is very important in preventing overuse injuries deep in the back of the ankle as well as avoiding blisters on your toe knuckles in your pointe shoes!

Level 1

1. Place a small soft ball against the wall, and sit facing it with legs extended. Pointe the ankle so the ball of the foot presses into the ball, but keep the toes pulled back. I.e. to a demi-pointe position on the ball.

2. Slowly pointe the toes, pressing the pads of them onto the ball keeping the toes long. Check that you can see the knuckles of each toe, and that the toes are not curled under. The ball will provide resistance so that you can really feel the small muscles under the foot working.

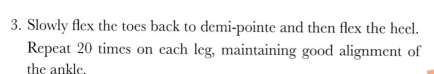

3. Slowly flex the toes back to demi-pointe and then flex the heel. Repeat 20 times on each leg, maintaining good alignment of the ankle.

Level 2

1. Repeat the exercise but keep the big toe pulled back as you pointe all the other toes onto the ball. Pause in this position, then slowly point the big toe.

2. Slowly flex the big toe, keeping the other toes pointed. Pause, then slowly flex the rest of the toes, keeping the ankle pointed, and then flex the heel. Repeat 20 times.

Sylvie Feet

This can be a tricky exercise to master, but it is fabulous for strengthening all of the small individual toe muscles as well as working your turnout muscles in your hip. It is named after Sylvie Guillem, who apparently does hundreds of these per day. She is an extraordinary dancer and it is this discipline and attention to detail that makes dancers like her so successful.

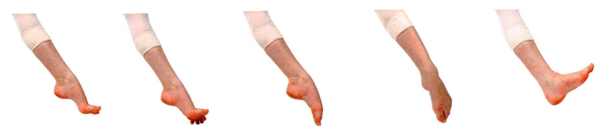

1. Stand side on to the barre in fifth position. Tendu the outside foot to second position keeping your hips square. Rotate the top of the thigh bones in their sockets to maintain turnout on both legs. Keeping the ankle pointed, flex all of the toes.

2. Turn out the working leg a little more and then place the pinkie toe down on the floor. Slowly place each consecutive toe to the floor in order.

3. Rotate the hip inwards in the socket then flex your foot. Keep the foot flexed and turn the leg back out in the socket.

4. Repeat three times before closing the leg behind. Finish with two tendu to second, before turnout and repeating on the other side.

Note:
- You should not feel any pain or discomfort behind the ankle in this exercise
- Keep your hips square to the front throughout this exercise. When done properly, it really works your whole body!

FDL Massage

If you have been scrunching your toes then this massage should help to release some tension that may have built up. Once the old tension has been released, it is much easier to start working you foot more correctly. The muscle belly of your FDL is deep up on the inside of your calf.

1. The best way to find your FDL is by seeing which muscle works when you scrunch your toes. Place your fingers deep up on the inside of your calf and curl then relax your toes. You should be able to feel one deep muscle tightening and releasing under your fingers. This is the one you want to massage.

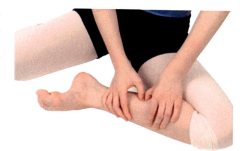

2. Slowly massage up this part of your calf with smooth slow strokes using either your fingers or the heel of your hand. Note any points of tension and slowly work through them. Try not to force your way through the muscle, but rather wait for the muscle to release before you move on.

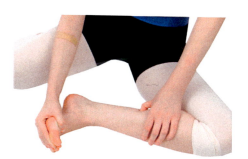

3. You can also use your thumb to work into any tender points you find, or use the trigger point charts (right) for some good spots to try.

Note:
- Sometimes this muscle is placed a little to the outer part of the leg rather than the inner surface
- Do not press into any very painful points for too long. Aim to feel the muscle release under your fingers
- If it is not letting go, use less pressure or move on to another point

FDL Stretch

The FDL stretch is very similar to the Tibialis Posterior stretch that we did earlier in the course. You stabilise the muscle by holding it with one hand, and then flex the foot to apply the stretch. A good stretch can also be gained by placing a rolled up towel under the ball of the foot in a soleus stretch.

1. Sit on the ground with the leg turned in, and the other turned out. With one finger, gently apply pressure to the FDL muscle. Remember to test that you have the right muscle by curling and relaxing the toes a few times.

2. Using the other hand slowly flex the toes back before flexing the heel and then releasing the stretch.

3. Repeat 3 times feeling the muscle glide under your fingers to give the FDL a gentle stretch.

4. Repeat on the other leg. Follow with a gentle calf stretch, or for even more benefit, a Soleus stretch with a rolled up towel under the ball of the foot.

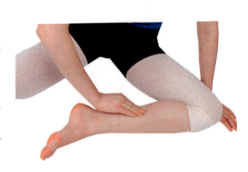

Note:
- This technique can release a lot of tension around the back of the calf that may be stopping the other muscles around this area from working properly
- Try a few tendus and rises after you have performed it on one foot to see what difference it makes for you

Notes:

Summary

So that is it! Just about everything you need to know about your feet and ankles as a dancer. We hope that you enjoy this course as much as we have putting it together!
There is so much information in this book, and also on our dedicated website to really help you take your dancing to the next level. Please make sure to contact us if you do not have access to the members area of this site. There is a wealth of information about using this program for healing different injuries and videos of each section.

Any questions that you may have about the program or the other resources can be sent to info@theballetblog.com and we will get back to you as soon as possible.

So, with all of this information, how do you integrate all this is your training?
This course is not designed to be done all at once. You can pick and chose certain areas to focus on at different points in time depending on what your needs are.
For example:
- If you are about to do a variation with lots of hops en pointe, then focus on the Soleus section.
- If you tend to sickle in when on demi-pointe, then focus on the section for strengthening your Peroneal muscles.
- If you know that you claw your toes when pointing your foot, then focus on the intrinsic foot muscle section.

This course is designed to give you all the information to really get to know your own feet. As you begin to master each section, you will notice big differences in your dancing, and before long your teachers should be noticing too!
Your journey with dance is a lifelong adventure of learning. Don't get bogged down with thinking that you have to learn all of the anatomy at once. Let it sink in and you may be surprised at just how easy it is to learn!

Kindest Regards,

Lisa Howell

Example of Soleus Program	M	T	W	T	F	S	S
Soleus Rises En Fondu							
Preparation for Petit Jeté							
Fondu Exercise on Demi Pointe							
Soleus Massage							
Soleus Stretch							

Example of Peroneal Program	M	T	W	T	F	S	S
Pointe through Demi-Pointe w. Resistance Band							
Resistance Band Rises with Transfers							
Resistance Band Rises with Transfers - V1							
Resistance Band Rises with Transfers - V2							
Resistance Band Rises with Transfers - V3							
Peroneal Massage							
Peroneal Stretch							

Example of Intrinsic Foot Muscles Program	M	T	W	T	F	S	S
Doming							
Toe Swapping							
Piano Playing							
Intrinsic Foot Massage							
Intrinsic Foot Stretch							

Acknowledgements

Thank you so much to every single client I have ever worked with. Your uniqueness, challenges and feedback have helped me hone our programs to be the most effective and efficient way of dealing with common issues, with enough customisation to ensure great results for everyone.

Huge thanks must also go to the hundreds of dance teachers worldwide who have attended my Teacher Training courses, and given such positive feedback on the application of these programs. I thrive off the feedback you give me and and your infectious enthusiasm inspires me to keep on giving.

Lisa xx

To gain access to the online video course that is the companion to this book please visit www.theballetblog.com. This course has videos of all of the exercises in much greater detail, as well as access to a bonus video and other features.

Related Resources

The Perfect Pointe Book

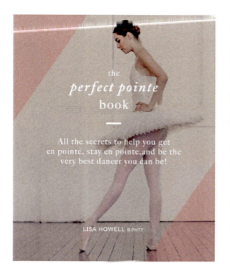

This unique book gives you the extra help you need to really get strong enough for pointe work. It includes lots of exercises, divided into four simple stages to work on the flexibility of your feet and ankles, the strength of your little foot muscles, your turnout and your core control. It also guides you through tests for each stage so that you can work out where your problem areas are! This book is essential for any student preparing for, or already en pointe, an any teacher wanting to learn more about safely preparing students for the most beautiful of dance forms!

Injury Management Guides

This series of Injury Management Guides is designed to help you understand any injury and empower you in managing your rehabilitation. Every dancer is different, and even two people diagnosed with the same injury may have totally different causes and rehab plans. The huge amount of information included on injury prevention make them a great resource for Dance Teachers who want to help the dancers in their care achieve their dreams without compromising their short term or long term physical health. The guides may also help health professionals convey more information to their clients in a shorter period of time, as well as understanding the complexity of rehabilitation of a dancer to full performance standard.

Made in the USA
San Bernardino, CA
20 May 2019